Welcome!

This Biblical Meditation Series is designed to help you meditate through the entire Bible in about three years. The series will help you read through each chapter of the Bible at a pace that allows you to meditate, apply, pray, and enjoy your time in the Word. At the end of the series, you will have created your own personal commentary of your time spent in the Bible.

The series continues with Volume Four. In this volume we will read through the books of Acts, Joshua, Romans, Judges, and Ruth as we work through the Bible alternating Old and New Testament books. Each volume will take you through approximately a quarter of a year but can be started at any time or with any book of the Bible.

Each day you work in this book, you will read the chapter (or short chapters) written at the top of the page, then you'll fill in each of the boxes on the two-page spread for that day. There are six days of regular work, then on the seventh day there are two pages for reflection on the previous week's work.

ABOUT THE DAILY QUESTIONS

In each daily spread you'll see questions going down the left side of the boxes and different ones on the right. Choose which set of questions you'll answer depending on the chapter. If there is a verse that really stands out in the chapter, then use the questions on the left. If the chapter is more narrative in structure (tells a story) then use the questions on the right. If neither of these apply, use the bookmark on the next page.

My hope and prayer is that as you work through these pages you'll have time to slow down and think deeply about the truth in the Bible and what it teachs about God and His redemptive plan and how it applies to your life and your growth as His child.

Visit me on my blog at www.StoneSoupForFive.com

Photo credit: Kendra Harvey
@Ledbystillwaters on Instagram

All maps taken from The Graphic Bible by Lewis Browne
now in the public domain

Cut out and use this bookmark for the hard, descriptive chapters.

You'll still be able to think through the chapter in a different way!

If you'd like a printable copy (to print on cardstock) you can find the file at my website under subscriber bonuses.

www.stonesoupforfive.com

Bible Reading and Meditation Journal

the hard chapters

Summarize
(keep this box the same)

I notice...
(replaces: Verses that stood out, box two)
Write out anything you notice
in the chapter. Anything at all.

I wonder...
(replaces: Why did I pick this verse, box three)
Is there anything you are curious about?
Anything you don't understand?
Anything you wonder about in the chapter?

I'm reminded of...
(replaces: Definitions of words, box four)
Were you reminded of anything when
you read through the chapter?
A story (real life or in the Bible)?
A verse?

Continue with the rest
of the boxes as written
(using the questions
on the right of box five).

www.stonesoupforfive.com

Word cloud courtesy of Blue Letter Bible
BlueLetterBible.org

the book of Acts preview

Before you start diving into a new book of the Bible, take sometime to learn about it, where it fits into the overall narrative of the Bible, and key themes to look for.

At the beginning of each new book of the Bible, I've included two preview pages for you to use to journal and take notes.

Read the introduction to the book of Acts in your Bible and jot down any notes.

There are some EXCELLENT videos on TheBibleProject.com or on their YouTube channel. On their website you can even print out a copy of their drawing (I shrink it down and print it out and tape it into my guide on the preview page). View the videos on the Bible project and also read the introduction at the beginning of the book in your Bible. They also have lots of other great resources, including podcasts talking about books of the Bible, so spend some time browsing around their site.

If you want to go even further, there are great free commentaries online to look up too. Here are some I love:

From Grace to You:
https://www.gty.org/library/bible-introductions

From Precept Austin:
http://www.preceptaustin.org/bybook

and Blue Letter Bible:
https://www.blueletterbible.org/resources/intros.cfm

Also, take a few moments to pray before you start your study:

my prayer

Father,

I want to know you more.
I want your truth written on my heart.
Thank you, for what you will
provide - more than I can ask
& even imagine.

Acts preview notes

Luke is the author
- physician
- missionary
- probably a gentile

Overview : how Jesus' followers were empowered & guided
by the Holy Spirit to take the Gospel
from Jerusalem to the ends of the earth

Audience - Christians, predominately Gentile churches
needing assurance of their identity
as children of God

Purpose - records what Jesus continues to do

"Paul's first missionary journey was about 1400 miles long—
approximately the distance from London to Brussels via Paris and return,
or from San Francisco to Salt Lake City and back."

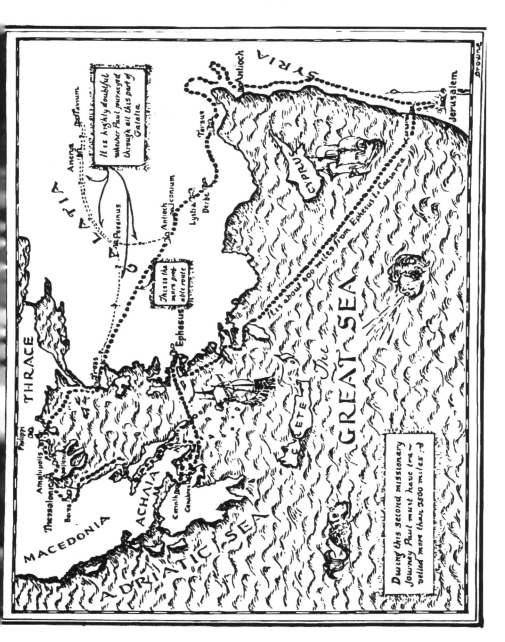

"During this second missionary journey Paul must have travelled more than 3,500 miles."

11

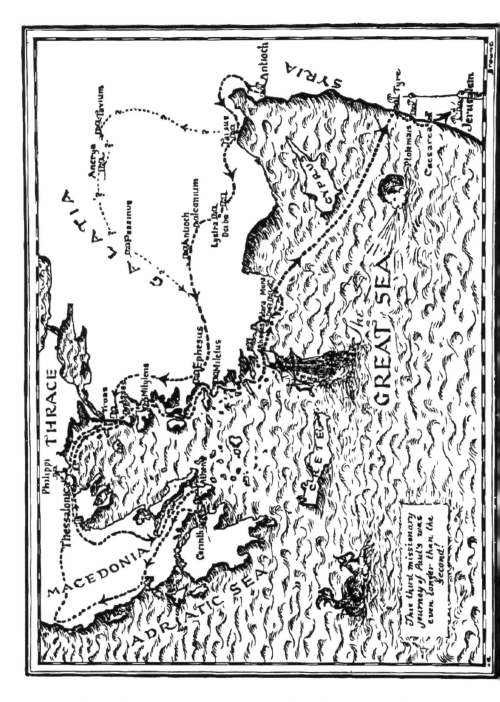

"This third missionary journey of Paul's was even longer than the second"

Acts preview notes

Acts 1

Date:

Summarize the main idea(s) in this chapter:

Verse(s) that stood out   or   Who is in this chapter?
What do they say? What do they do?

Why did I pick this verse?   or   What is going on?
Is there anything going wrong?

Definitions of words and/or   or   When and where
cross references from my verse   did this happen?

Rewrite the passage in your own words   or   Why is this chapter in the Bible?
or personalize it.   Why did these events happen?
                                                                            Why did the people act this way?

Does this reveal anything about God/Jesus/Holy Spirit?
Are there examples to follow or avoid? What does this chapter have to teach me?

How can I apply insights from this today? This week?

Notes, quotes, doodles, checklists, prayers, etc.

15

Acts 2

Date:

Summarize the main idea(s) in this chapter:

Verse(s) that stood out   or   Who is in this chapter?
What do they say? What do they do?

Why did I pick this verse?   or   What is going on?
Is there anything going wrong?

Definitions of words and/or   or   When and where
cross references from my verse   did this happen?

Rewrite the passage in your own words   or   Why is this chapter in the Bible?
or personalize it.   Why did these events happen?
                                                   Why did the people act this way?

Does this reveal anything about God/Jesus/Holy Spirit?
Are there examples to follow or avoid? What does this chapter have to teach me?

How can I apply insights from this today? This week?

Notes, quotes, doodles, checklists, prayers, etc.

17

Acts 3

Date:

Summarize the main idea(s) in this chapter:

Verse(s) that stood out   or   Who is in this chapter?
What do they say? What do they do?

Why did I pick this verse?   or   What is going on?
Is there anything going wrong?

Definitions of words and/or   or   When and where
cross references from my verse   did this happen?

Rewrite the passage in your own words   or   Why is this chapter in the Bible?
or personalize it.   Why did these events happen?
                                                             Why did the people act this way?

Does this reveal anything about God/Jesus/Holy Spirit?
Are there examples to follow or avoid? What does this chapter have to teach me?

How can I apply insights from this today? This week?

Notes, quotes, doodles, checklists, prayers, etc.

19

Acts 4

Date:

Summarize the main idea(s) in this chapter:

Verse(s) that stood out   or   Who is in this chapter?
What do they say? What do they do?

Why did I pick this verse?   or   What is going on?
Is there anything going wrong?

Definitions of words and/or   or   When and where
cross references from my verse   did this happen?

Rewrite the passage in your own words
or personalize it.

or

Why is this chapter in the Bible?
Why did these events happen?
Why did the people act this way?

Does this reveal anything about God/Jesus/Holy Spirit?
Are there examples to follow or avoid? What does this chapter have to teach me?

How can I apply insights from this today? This week?

Notes, quotes, doodles, checklists, prayers, etc.

#Iwillmeditate

Acts 5

Date:

Summarize the main idea(s) in this chapter:

Verse(s) that stood out   or   Who is in this chapter?
What do they say? What do they do?

Why did I pick this verse?   or   What is going on?
Is there anything going wrong?

Definitions of words and/or   or   When and where
cross references from my verse   did this happen?

Rewrite the passage in your own words   or   Why is this chapter in the Bible?
or personalize it.   Why did these events happen?
Why did the people act this way?

Does this reveal anything about God/Jesus/Holy Spirit?
Are there examples to follow or avoid? What does this chapter have to teach me?

How can I apply insights from this today? This week?

Notes, quotes, doodles, checklists, prayers, etc.

Acts 6

Date:

Summarize the main idea(s) in this chapter:

Verse(s) that stood out   or   Who is in this chapter?
What do they say? What do they do?

Why did I pick this verse?   or   What is going on?
Is there anything going wrong?

Definitions of words and/or
cross references from my verse   or   When and where
did this happen?

Rewrite the passage in your own words   or   Why is this chapter in the Bible?
or personalize it.   Why did these events happen?
                                                      Why did the people act this way?

Does this reveal anything about God/Jesus/Holy Spirit?
Are there examples to follow or avoid? What does this chapter have to teach me?

How can I apply insights from this today? This week?

Notes, quotes, doodles, checklists, prayers, etc.

Review and reflect

Date:

Review each of the last six days work. Write or list the main takeaway you got from each chapter. (Look closely at the sections "What does this reveal about God?" and "How can I apply this?")

Are there any themes showing up in this week's work?

Are there any areas God is wanting to grow my faith or trust?
Are there any insights from this week's work on how to do this?

Are there any sins God is spotlighting in my life?
Are there any insights from this week's work on how to kill these sins?

Re-read one or two of the most impactful verses from this week and turn them into a prayer. (There is room on the next pages to write it down if you want.)

How can I thank or praise God as a result of what I've learned this week?

How can I apply what I've learned this week to my life today and next week?

Where do I need His strength for today? Tomorrow? Next week?

Is there a verse from this week that I should commit to memory? Write it on the next page or on a 3x5 card to take with you to memorize.

Are there any sins I need to confess to God in prayer?

Is there anyone I need to forgive? Is there anyone I need to ask forgiveness of?

Are there any seeds of bitterness starting to take root in my heart?

Are there any fears or worries I need to lay at His feet?

notes, verses to memorize

prayers, doodles, etc

☐ pray before beginning
☐ review what came before

Acts 7

Date:

Summarize the main idea(s) in this chapter:

Verse(s) that stood out   or   Who is in this chapter?
What do they say? What do they do?

Why did I pick this verse?   or   What is going on?
Is there anything going wrong?

Definitions of words and/or   or   When and where
cross references from my verse   did this happen?

Rewrite the passage in your own words   or   Why is this chapter in the Bible?
or personalize it.   Why did these events happen?
                                                                                         Why did the people act this way?

Does this reveal anything about God/Jesus/Holy Spirit?
Are there examples to follow or avoid? What does this chapter have to teach me?

How can I apply insights from this today? This week?

Notes, quotes, doodles, checklists, prayers, etc.

☐ pray before beginning
☐ review what came before

Acts 8

Date:

Summarize the main idea(s) in this chapter:

Verse(s) that stood out   or   Who is in this chapter?
What do they say? What do they do?

Why did I pick this verse?   or   What is going on?
Is there anything going wrong?

Definitions of words and/or   or   When and where
cross references from my verse   did this happen?

Rewrite the passage in your own words   or   Why is this chapter in the Bible?
or personalize it.   Why did these events happen?
                                                                   Why did the people act this way?

Does this reveal anything about God/Jesus/Holy Spirit?
Are there examples to follow or avoid? What does this chapter have to teach me?

How can I apply insights from this today? This week?

Notes, quotes, doodles, checklists, prayers, etc.

Acts 9

Date:

Summarize the main idea(s) in this chapter:

Verse(s) that stood out   or   Who is in this chapter?
What do they say? What do they do?

Why did I pick this verse?   or   What is going on?
Is there anything going wrong?

Definitions of words and/or   or   When and where
cross references from my verse   did this happen?

Rewrite the passage in your own words   or   Why is this chapter in the Bible?
or personalize it.   Why did these events happen?
                                                                                  Why did the people act this way?

Does this reveal anything about God/Jesus/Holy Spirit?
Are there examples to follow or avoid? What does this chapter have to teach me?

How can I apply insights from this today? This week?

Notes, quotes, doodles, checklists, prayers, etc.

35

Acts 10

Date:

Summarize the main idea(s) in this chapter:

Verse(s) that stood out   or   Who is in this chapter?
What do they say? What do they do?

Why did I pick this verse?   or   What is going on?
Is there anything going wrong?

Definitions of words and/or   or   When and where
cross references from my verse   did this happen?

Rewrite the passage in your own words   or   Why is this chapter in the Bible?
or personalize it.   Why did these events happen?
                                                                      Why did the people act this way?

Does this reveal anything about God/Jesus/Holy Spirit?
Are there examples to follow or avoid? What does this chapter have to teach me?

How can I apply insights from this today? This week?

Notes, quotes, doodles, checklists, prayers, etc.

Acts 11

Date:

Summarize the main idea(s) in this chapter:

Verse(s) that stood out   or   Who is in this chapter?
What do they say? What do they do?

Why did I pick this verse?   or   What is going on?
Is there anything going wrong?

Definitions of words and/or   or   When and where
cross references from my verse   did this happen?

Rewrite the passage in your own words   or   Why is this chapter in the Bible?
or personalize it.   Why did these events happen?
                                                                                 Why did the people act this way?

Does this reveal anything about God/Jesus/Holy Spirit?
Are there examples to follow or avoid? What does this chapter have to teach me?

How can I apply insights from this today? This week?

Notes, quotes, doodles, checklists, prayers, etc.

39

☐ pray before beginning
☐ review what came before

Acts 12

Date:

Summarize the main idea(s) in this chapter:

Verse(s) that stood out   or   Who is in this chapter?
What do they say? What do they do?

Why did I pick this verse?   or   What is going on?
Is there anything going wrong?

Definitions of words and/or   or   When and where
cross references from my verse   did this happen?

Rewrite the passage in your own words   or   Why is this chapter in the Bible?
or personalize it.   Why did these events happen?
                                                                   Why did the people act this way?

Does this reveal anything about God/Jesus/Holy Spirit?
Are there examples to follow or avoid? What does this chapter have to teach me?

How can I apply insights from this today? This week?

Notes, quotes, doodles, checklists, prayers, etc.

41

☐ pray before beginning

Review and reflect

Date:

Review each of the last six days work. Write or list the main takeaway you got from each chapter. (Look closely at the sections "What does this reveal about God?" and "How can I apply this?")

Are there any themes showing up in this week's work?

Are there any areas God is wanting to grow my faith or trust?
Are there any insights from this week's work on how to do this?

Are there any sins God is spotlighting in my life?
Are there any insights from this week's work on how to kill these sins?

Re-read one or two of the most impactful verses from this week and turn them into a prayer. (There is room on the next pages to write it down if you want.)

How can I thank or praise God as a result of what I've learned this week?

How can I apply what I've learned this week to my life today and next week?

Where do I need His strength for today? Tomorrow? Next week?

Is there a verse from this week that I should commit to memory? Write it on the next page or on a 3x5 card to take with you to memorize.

Are there any sins I need to confess to God in prayer?

Is there anyone I need to forgive? Is there anyone I need to ask forgiveness of?

Are there any seeds of bitterness starting to take root in my heart?

Are there any fears or worries I need to lay at His feet?

#Iwillmeditate

notes, verses to memorize

prayers, doodles, etc

Acts 13

Date:

Summarize the main idea(s) in this chapter:

Verse(s) that stood out   or   Who is in this chapter?
What do they say? What do they do?

Why did I pick this verse?   or   What is going on?
Is there anything going wrong?

Definitions of words and/or   or   When and where
cross references from my verse   did this happen?

Rewrite the passage in your own words   or   Why is this chapter in the Bible?
or personalize it.   Why did these events happen?
                                                                    Why did the people act this way?

Does this reveal anything about God/Jesus/Holy Spirit?
Are there examples to follow or avoid? What does this chapter have to teach me?

How can I apply insights from this today? This week?

Notes, quotes, doodles, checklists, prayers, etc.

#Iwillmeditate

☐ pray before beginning
☐ review what came before

Acts 14

Date:

Summarize the main idea(s) in this chapter:

Verse(s) that stood out   or   Who is in this chapter?
What do they say? What do they do?

Why did I pick this verse?   or   What is going on?
Is there anything going wrong?

Definitions of words and/or   or   When and where
cross references from my verse   did this happen?

Rewrite the passage in your own words   or   Why is this chapter in the Bible?
or personalize it.   Why did these events happen?
                                                         Why did the people act this way?

Does this reveal anything about God/Jesus/Holy Spirit?
Are there examples to follow or avoid? What does this chapter have to teach me?

How can I apply insights from this today? This week?

Notes, quotes, doodles, checklists, prayers, etc.

49

Acts 15

Date:

Summarize the main idea(s) in this chapter:

Verse(s) that stood out   or   Who is in this chapter?
What do they say? What do they do?

Why did I pick this verse?   or   What is going on?
Is there anything going wrong?

Definitions of words and/or   or   When and where
cross references from my verse   did this happen?

Rewrite the passage in your own words   or   Why is this chapter in the Bible?
or personalize it.   Why did these events happen?
                                                                          Why did the people act this way?

Does this reveal anything about God/Jesus/Holy Spirit?
Are there examples to follow or avoid? What does this chapter have to teach me?

How can I apply insights from this today? This week?

Notes, quotes, doodles, checklists, prayers, etc.

51

Acts 16

Date:

Summarize the main idea(s) in this chapter:

Verse(s) that stood out   or   Who is in this chapter?
What do they say? What do they do?

Why did I pick this verse?   or   What is going on?
Is there anything going wrong?

Definitions of words and/or   or   When and where
cross references from my verse   did this happen?

Rewrite the passage in your own words   or   Why is this chapter in the Bible?
or personalize it.   Why did these events happen?
                                                Why did the people act this way?

Does this reveal anything about God/Jesus/Holy Spirit?
Are there examples to follow or avoid? What does this chapter have to teach me?

How can I apply insights from this today? This week?

Notes, quotes, doodles, checklists, prayers, etc.

#Iwillmeditate

☐ pray before beginning
☐ review what came before

Acts 17

Date:

Summarize the main idea(s) in this chapter:

Verse(s) that stood out   or   Who is in this chapter?
What do they say? What do they do?

Why did I pick this verse?   or   What is going on?
Is there anything going wrong?

Definitions of words and/or   or   When and where
cross references from my verse   did this happen?

Rewrite the passage in your own words   or   Why is this chapter in the Bible?
or personalize it.   Why did these events happen?
                                                                           Why did the people act this way?

Does this reveal anything about God/Jesus/Holy Spirit?
Are there examples to follow or avoid? What does this chapter have to teach me?

How can I apply insights from this today? This week?

Notes, quotes, doodles, checklists, prayers, etc.

☐ pray before beginning
☐ review what came before

Acts 18

Date:

Summarize the main idea(s) in this chapter:

Verse(s) that stood out   or   Who is in this chapter?
What do they say? What do they do?

Why did I pick this verse?   or   What is going on?
Is there anything going wrong?

Definitions of words and/or   or   When and where
cross references from my verse   did this happen?

Rewrite the passage in your own words   or   Why is this chapter in the Bible?
or personalize it.   Why did these events happen?
                                                                     Why did the people act this way?

Does this reveal anything about God/Jesus/Holy Spirit?
Are there examples to follow or avoid? What does this chapter have to teach me?

How can I apply insights from this today? This week?

Notes, quotes, doodles, checklists, prayers, etc.

Review and reflect

Date:

Review each of the last six days work. Write or list the main takeaway you got from each chapter. (Look closely at the sections "What does this reveal about God?" and "How can I apply this?")

Are there any themes showing up in this week's work?

Are there any areas God is wanting to grow my faith or trust?
Are there any insights from this week's work on how to do this?

Are there any sins God is spotlighting in my life?
Are there any insights from this week's work on how to kill these sins?

Re-read one or two of the most impactful verses from this week and turn them into a prayer. (There is room on the next pages to write it down if you want.)

How can I thank or praise God as a result of what I've learned this week?

How can I apply what I've learned this week to my life today and next week?

Where do I need His strength for today? Tomorrow? Next week?

Is there a verse from this week that I should commit to memory? Write it on the next page or on a 3x5 card to take with you to memorize.

Are there any sins I need to confess to God in prayer?

Is there anyone I need to forgive? Is there anyone I need to ask forgiveness of?

Are there any seeds of bitterness starting to take root in my heart?

Are there any fears or worries I need to lay at His feet?

notes, verses to memorize

prayers, doodles, etc

Acts 19

Date:

Summarize the main idea(s) in this chapter:

Verse(s) that stood out   or   Who is in this chapter?
What do they say? What do they do?

Why did I pick this verse?   or   What is going on?
Is there anything going wrong?

Definitions of words and/or   or   When and where
cross references from my verse   did this happen?

Rewrite the passage in your own words   or   Why is this chapter in the Bible?
or personalize it.   Why did these events happen?
                                                 Why did the people act this way?

Does this reveal anything about God/Jesus/Holy Spirit?
Are there examples to follow or avoid? What does this chapter have to teach me?

How can I apply insights from this today? This week?

Notes, quotes, doodles, checklists, prayers, etc.

Acts 20

Date:

Summarize the main idea(s) in this chapter:

Verse(s) that stood out   or   Who is in this chapter?
What do they say? What do they do?

Why did I pick this verse?   or   What is going on?
Is there anything going wrong?

Definitions of words and/or   or   When and where
cross references from my verse   did this happen?

Rewrite the passage in your own words   or   Why is this chapter in the Bible?
or personalize it.   Why did these events happen?
                                                            Why did the people act this way?

Does this reveal anything about God/Jesus/Holy Spirit?
Are there examples to follow or avoid? What does this chapter have to teach me?

How can I apply insights from this today? This week?

Notes, quotes, doodles, checklists, prayers, etc.

65

Acts 21

Date:

Summarize the main idea(s) in this chapter:

Verse(s) that stood out   or   Who is in this chapter?
What do they say? What do they do?

Why did I pick this verse?   or   What is going on?
Is there anything going wrong?

Definitions of words and/or   or   When and where
cross references from my verse   did this happen?

Rewrite the passage in your own words   or   Why is this chapter in the Bible?
or personalize it.   Why did these events happen?
                                                                            Why did the people act this way?

Does this reveal anything about God/Jesus/Holy Spirit?
Are there examples to follow or avoid? What does this chapter have to teach me?

How can I apply insights from this today? This week?

Notes, quotes, doodles, checklists, prayers, etc.

67

Acts 22

Date:

Summarize the main idea(s) in this chapter:

Verse(s) that stood out   or   Who is in this chapter?
What do they say? What do they do?

Why did I pick this verse?   or   What is going on?
Is there anything going wrong?

Definitions of words and/or   or   When and where
cross references from my verse   did this happen?

Rewrite the passage in your own words or personalize it.   or   Why is this chapter in the Bible?
Why did these events happen?
Why did the people act this way?

Does this reveal anything about God/Jesus/Holy Spirit?
Are there examples to follow or avoid? What does this chapter have to teach me?

How can I apply insights from this today? This week?

Notes, quotes, doodles, checklists, prayers, etc.

#Iwillmeditate

☐ pray before beginning
☐ review what came before

Acts 23

Date:

Summarize the main idea(s) in this chapter:

Verse(s) that stood out   or   Who is in this chapter?
What do they say? What do they do?

Why did I pick this verse?   or   What is going on?
Is there anything going wrong?

Definitions of words and/or   or   When and where
cross references from my verse   did this happen?

Rewrite the passage in your own words   or   Why is this chapter in the Bible?
or personalize it.   Why did these events happen?
                                                Why did the people act this way?

Does this reveal anything about God/Jesus/Holy Spirit?
Are there examples to follow or avoid? What does this chapter have to teach me?

How can I apply insights from this today? This week?

Notes, quotes, doodles, checklists, prayers, etc.

Acts 24

Date:

Summarize the main idea(s) in this chapter:

Verse(s) that stood out   or   Who is in this chapter?
                                              What do they say? What do they do?

Why did I pick this verse?   or   What is going on?
                                              Is there anything going wrong?

Definitions of words and/or   or   When and where
cross references from my verse   did this happen?

Rewrite the passage in your own words or personalize it.

or

Why is this chapter in the Bible?
Why did these events happen?
Why did the people act this way?

Does this reveal anything about God/Jesus/Holy Spirit?
Are there examples to follow or avoid? What does this chapter have to teach me?

How can I apply insights from this today? This week?

Notes, quotes, doodles, checklists, prayers, etc.

Review and reflect

Date:

Review each of the last six days work. Write or list the main takeaway you got from each chapter. (Look closely at the sections "What does this reveal about God?" and "How can I apply this?")

Are there any themes showing up in this week's work?

Are there any areas God is wanting to grow my faith or trust?
Are there any insights from this week's work on how to do this?

Are there any sins God is spotlighting in my life?
Are there any insights from this week's work on how to kill these sins?

Re-read one or two of the most impactful verses from this week and turn them into a prayer. (There is room on the next pages to write it down if you want.)

How can I thank or praise God as a result of what I've learned this week?

How can I apply what I've learned this week to my life today and next week?

Where do I need His strength for today? Tomorrow? Next week?

Is there a verse from this week that I should commit to memory? Write it on the next page or on a 3x5 card to take with you to memorize.

Are there any sins I need to confess to God in prayer?

Is there anyone I need to forgive? Is there anyone I need to ask forgiveness of?

Are there any seeds of bitterness starting to take root in my heart?

Are there any fears or worries I need to lay at His feet?

#Iwillmeditate

notes, verses to memorize

prayers, doodles, etc

Acts 25

Date:

Summarize the main idea(s) in this chapter:

Verse(s) that stood out   or   Who is in this chapter?
What do they say? What do they do?

Why did I pick this verse?   or   What is going on?
Is there anything going wrong?

Definitions of words and/or   or   When and where
cross references from my verse   did this happen?

Rewrite the passage in your own words   or   Why is this chapter in the Bible?
or personalize it.   Why did these events happen?
                                                                       Why did the people act this way?

Does this reveal anything about God/Jesus/Holy Spirit?
Are there examples to follow or avoid? What does this chapter have to teach me?

How can I apply insights from this today? This week?

Notes, quotes, doodles, checklists, prayers, etc.

#Iwillmeditate

Acts 26

Date:

Summarize the main idea(s) in this chapter:

Verse(s) that stood out   or   Who is in this chapter?
What do they say? What do they do?

Why did I pick this verse?   or   What is going on?
Is there anything going wrong?

Definitions of words and/or   or   When and where
cross references from my verse   did this happen?

Rewrite the passage in your own words or personalize it.   or   Why is this chapter in the Bible? Why did these events happen? Why did the people act this way?

Does this reveal anything about God/Jesus/Holy Spirit?
Are there examples to follow or avoid? What does this chapter have to teach me?

How can I apply insights from this today? This week?

Notes, quotes, doodles, checklists, prayers, etc.

☐ pray before beginning
☐ review what came before

Acts 27

Date:

Summarize the main idea(s) in this chapter:

Verse(s) that stood out   or   Who is in this chapter?
What do they say? What do they do?

Why did I pick this verse?   or   What is going on?
Is there anything going wrong?

Definitions of words and/or   or   When and where
cross references from my verse   did this happen?

Rewrite the passage in your own words   or   Why is this chapter in the Bible?
or personalize it.   Why did these events happen?
                                                                 Why did the people act this way?

Does this reveal anything about God/Jesus/Holy Spirit?
Are there examples to follow or avoid? What does this chapter have to teach me?

How can I apply insights from this today? This week?

Notes, quotes, doodles, checklists, prayers, etc.

Acts 28

Date:

Summarize the main idea(s) in this chapter:

Verse(s) that stood out   or   Who is in this chapter?
What do they say? What do they do?

Why did I pick this verse?   or   What is going on?
Is there anything going wrong?

Definitions of words and/or
cross references from my verse   or   When and where
did this happen?

Rewrite the passage in your own words   or   Why is this chapter in the Bible?
or personalize it.   Why did these events happen?
                                                                      Why did the people act this way?

Does this reveal anything about God/Jesus/Holy Spirit?
Are there examples to follow or avoid? What does this chapter have to teach me?

How can I apply insights from this today? This week?

Notes, quotes, doodles, checklists, prayers, etc.

Review and reflect

Date:

Review each of the last six days work. Write or list the main takeaway you got from each chapter. (Look closely at the sections "What does this reveal about God?" and "How can I apply this?")

Are there any themes showing up in this week's work?

Are there any areas God is wanting to grow my faith or trust?
Are there any insights from this week's work on how to do this?

Are there any sins God is spotlighting in my life?
Are there any insights from this week's work on how to kill these sins?

Re-read one or two of the most impactful verses from this week and turn them into a prayer. (There is room on the next pages to write it down if you want.)

How can I thank or praise God as a result of what I've learned this week?

How can I apply what I've learned this week to my life today and next week?

Where do I need His strength for today? Tomorrow? Next week?

Is there a verse from this week that I should commit to memory? Write it on the next page or on a 3x5 card to take with you to memorize.

Are there any sins I need to confess to God in prayer?

Is there anyone I need to forgive? Is there anyone I need to ask forgiveness of?

Are there any seeds of bitterness starting to take root in my heart?

Are there any fears or worries I need to lay at His feet?

notes, verses to memorize

prayers, doodles, etc

the book of Joshua preview

Read the introduction to the book of Joshua in your Bible and jot down any notes.

There are some EXCELLENT videos on TheBibleProject.com or on their YouTube channel. On their website you can even print out a copy of their drawing (I shrink it down and print it out and tape it into my guide on the preview page). View the videos on the Bible project and also read the introduction at the beginning of the book in your Bible. They also have lots of other great resources, including podcasts talking about books of the Bible, so spend some time browsing around their site.

If you want to go even further, there are great free commentaries online to look up too. Here are some I love:

From Grace to You:
https://www.gty.org/library/bible-introductions

From Precept Austin:
http://www.preceptaustin.org/bybook

and Blue Letter Bible:
https://www.blueletterbible.org/resources/intros.cfm

Also, take a few moments to pray before you start your study:

my prayer

Joshua preview notes

1st half – conquest of the promised land
2nd – division of the land among the 12 tribes

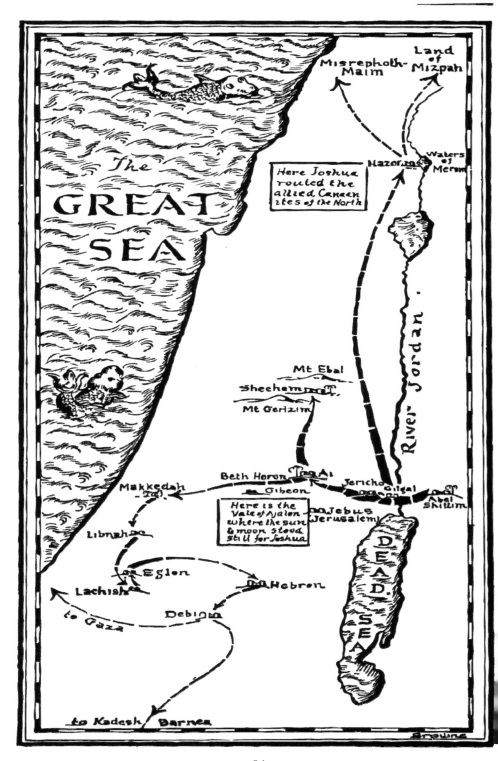

The GREAT SEA

Land of Mizpah

Misrepholh-Maim

Waters of Merom

Hazor

Here Joshua routed the allied Canaanites of the North

River Jordan

Mt Ebal

Shechem

Mt Gerizim

Beth Horon   Ai

Makkedah   Gibeon

Jericho   Gilgal

Abel Shittim

Here is the Vale of Ajalon where the sun & moon stood still for Joshua

Jebus (Jerusalem)

Libnah

Eglon

Lachish

Hebron

Debir

to Gaza

DEAD SEA

to Kadesh Barnea

Joshua preview notes

Joshua 1-2

Date:

Summarize the main idea(s) in this chapter:

Verse(s) that stood out   or   Who is in this chapter?
What do they say? What do they do?

Why did I pick this verse?   or   What is going on?
Is there anything going wrong?

Definitions of words and/or   or   When and where
cross references from my verse   did this happen?

Rewrite the passage in your own words or personalize it.

or

Why is this chapter in the Bible?
Why did these events happen?
Why did the people act this way?

Does this reveal anything about God/Jesus/Holy Spirit?
Are there examples to follow or avoid? What does this chapter have to teach me?

How can I apply insights from this today? This week?

Notes, quotes, doodles, checklists, prayers, etc.

#Iwillmeditate

Joshua 3-4

Date:

Summarize the main idea(s) in this chapter:

Verse(s) that stood out   or   Who is in this chapter?
What do they say? What do they do?

Why did I pick this verse?   or   What is going on?
Is there anything going wrong?

Definitions of words and/or   or   When and where
cross references from my verse   did this happen?

Rewrite the passage in your own words   or   Why is this chapter in the Bible?
or personalize it.   Why did these events happen?
                                                              Why did the people act this way?

Does this reveal anything about God/Jesus/Holy Spirit?
Are there examples to follow or avoid? What does this chapter have to teach me?

How can I apply insights from this today? This week?

Notes, quotes, doodles, checklists, prayers, etc.

Johsua 5-6

Date:

Summarize the main idea(s) in this chapter:

Verse(s) that stood out   or   Who is in this chapter?
What do they say? What do they do?

Why did I pick this verse?   or   What is going on?
Is there anything going wrong?

Definitions of words and/or   or   When and where
cross references from my verse   did this happen?

Rewrite the passage in your own words   or   Why is this chapter in the Bible?
or personalize it.   Why did these events happen?
                                                 Why did the people act this way?

Does this reveal anything about God/Jesus/Holy Spirit?
Are there examples to follow or avoid? What does this chapter have to teach me?

How can I apply insights from this today? This week?

Notes, quotes, doodles, checklists, prayers, etc.

#Iwillmeditate

Joshua 7

Date:

Summarize the main idea(s) in this chapter:

Verse(s) that stood out   or   Who is in this chapter?
What do they say? What do they do?

Why did I pick this verse?   or   What is going on?
Is there anything going wrong?

Definitions of words and/or   or   When and where
cross references from my verse   did this happen?

Rewrite the passage in your own words or personalize it.

or

Why is this chapter in the Bible?
Why did these events happen?
Why did the people act this way?

Does this reveal anything about God/Jesus/Holy Spirit?
Are there examples to follow or avoid? What does this chapter have to teach me?

How can I apply insights from this today? This week?

Notes, quotes, doodles, checklists, prayers, etc.

Joshua 8

Date:

Summarize the main idea(s) in this chapter:

Verse(s) that stood out   or   Who is in this chapter?
What do they say? What do they do?

Why did I pick this verse?   or   What is going on?
Is there anything going wrong?

Definitions of words and/or   or   When and where
cross references from my verse   did this happen?

Rewrite the passage in your own words   or   Why is this chapter in the Bible?
or personalize it.   Why did these events happen?
                                                Why did the people act this way?

Does this reveal anything about God/Jesus/Holy Spirit?
Are there examples to follow or avoid? What does this chapter have to teach me?

How can I apply insights from this today? This week?

Notes, quotes, doodles, checklists, prayers, etc.

☐ pray before beginning
☐ review what came before

Joshua 9

Date:

Summarize the main idea(s) in this chapter:

Verse(s) that stood out   or   Who is in this chapter? What do they say? What do they do?

Why did I pick this verse?   or   What is going on? Is there anything going wrong?

Definitions of words and/or cross references from my verse   or   When and where did this happen?

Rewrite the passage in your own words or personalize it.   or   Why is this chapter in the Bible?
Why did these events happen?
Why did the people act this way?

Does this reveal anything about God/Jesus/Holy Spirit?
Are there examples to follow or avoid? What does this chapter have to teach me?

How can I apply insights from this today? This week?

Notes, quotes, doodles, checklists, prayers, etc.

#Iwillmeditate

Review and reflect

Date:

Review each of the last six days work. Write or list the main takeaway you got from each chapter. (Look closely at the sections "What does this reveal about God?" and "How can I apply this?")

Are there any themes showing up in this week's work?

Are there any areas God is wanting to grow my faith or trust?
Are there any insights from this week's work on how to do this?

Are there any sins God is spotlighting in my life?
Are there any insights from this week's work on how to kill these sins?

Re-read one or two of the most impactful verses from this week and turn them into a prayer. (There is room on the next pages to write it down if you want.)

How can I thank or praise God as a result of what I've learned this week?

_____
_____
_____
_____
_____

How can I apply what I've learned this week to my life today and next week?

_____
_____
_____
_____
_____

Where do I need His strength for today? Tomorrow? Next week?

_____
_____
_____
_____
_____
_____
_____

Is there a verse from this week that I should commit to memory? Write it on the next page or on a 3x5 card to take with you to memorize.

Are there any sins I need to confess to God in prayer?

Is there anyone I need to forgive? Is there anyone I need to ask forgiveness of?

Are there any seeds of bitterness starting to take root in my heart?

Are there any fears or worries I need to lay at His feet?

notes, verses to memorize

prayers, doodles, etc

☐ pray before beginning
☐ review what came before

Joshua 10

Date:

Summarize the main idea(s) in this chapter:

Verse(s) that stood out   or   Who is in this chapter?
What do they say? What do they do?

Why did I pick this verse?   or   What is going on?
Is there anything going wrong?

Definitions of words and/or   or   When and where
cross references from my verse   did this happen?

112

Rewrite the passage in your own words or personalize it.   or

Why is this chapter in the Bible?
Why did these events happen?
Why did the people act this way?

Does this reveal anything about God/Jesus/Holy Spirit?
Are there examples to follow or avoid? What does this chapter have to teach me?

How can I apply insights from this today? This week?

Notes, quotes, doodles, checklists, prayers, etc.

Joshua 11-12

Date:

Summarize the main idea(s) in this chapter:

Verse(s) that stood out   or   Who is in this chapter?
What do they say? What do they do?

Why did I pick this verse?   or   What is going on?
Is there anything going wrong?

Definitions of words and/or   or   When and where
cross references from my verse   did this happen?

Rewrite the passage in your own words   or   Why is this chapter in the Bible?
or personalize it.   Why did these events happen?
                                                                       Why did the people act this way?

Does this reveal anything about God/Jesus/Holy Spirit?
Are there examples to follow or avoid? What does this chapter have to teach me?

How can I apply insights from this today? This week?

Notes, quotes, doodles, checklists, prayers, etc.

#Iwillmeditate

Joshua 13-14

Date:

Summarize the main idea(s) in this chapter:

Verse(s) that stood out   or   Who is in this chapter?
What do they say? What do they do?

Why did I pick this verse?   or   What is going on?
Is there anything going wrong?

Definitions of words and/or   or   When and where
cross references from my verse   did this happen?

Rewrite the passage in your own words   or   Why is this chapter in the Bible?
or personalize it.   Why did these events happen?
                                                                     Why did the people act this way?

Does this reveal anything about God/Jesus/Holy Spirit?
Are there examples to follow or avoid? What does this chapter have to teach me?

How can I apply insights from this today? This week?

Notes, quotes, doodles, checklists, prayers, etc.

Joshua 15

Date:

Summarize the main idea(s) in this chapter:

Verse(s) that stood out   or   Who is in this chapter?
What do they say? What do they do?

Why did I pick this verse?   or   What is going on?
Is there anything going wrong?

Definitions of words and/or   or   When and where
cross references from my verse   did this happen?

Rewrite the passage in your own words   or   Why is this chapter in the Bible?
or personalize it.   Why did these events happen?
                                                            Why did the people act this way?

Does this reveal anything about God/Jesus/Holy Spirit?
Are there examples to follow or avoid? What does this chapter have to teach me?

How can I apply insights from this today? This week?

Notes, quotes, doodles, checklists, prayers, etc.

Joshua 16-17

Date:

Summarize the main idea(s) in this chapter:

Verse(s) that stood out   or   Who is in this chapter?
                                                What do they say? What do they do?

Why did I pick this verse?   or   What is going on?
                                                Is there anything going wrong?

Definitions of words and/or   or   When and where
cross references from my verse   did this happen?

Rewrite the passage in your own words   or   Why is this chapter in the Bible?
or personalize it.   Why did these events happen?
                                                                                   Why did the people act this way?

Does this reveal anything about God/Jesus/Holy Spirit?
Are there examples to follow or avoid? What does this chapter have to teach me?

How can I apply insights from this today? This week?

Notes, quotes, doodles, checklists, prayers, etc.

#Iwillmeditate

☐ pray before beginning
☐ review what came before

Joshua 18

Date:

Summarize the main idea(s) in this chapter:

Verse(s) that stood out   or   Who is in this chapter?
What do they say? What do they do?

Why did I pick this verse?   or   What is going on?
Is there anything going wrong?

Definitions of words and/or   or   When and where
cross references from my verse   did this happen?

Rewrite the passage in your own words   or   Why is this chapter in the Bible?
or personalize it.   Why did these events happen?
                                                                Why did the people act this way?

Does this reveal anything about God/Jesus/Holy Spirit?
Are there examples to follow or avoid? What does this chapter have to teach me?

How can I apply insights from this today? This week?

Notes, quotes, doodles, checklists, prayers, etc.

123

Review and reflect

Date:

Review each of the last six days work. Write or list the main takeaway you got from each chapter. (Look closely at the sections "What does this reveal about God?" and "How can I apply this?")

Are there any themes showing up in this week's work?

Are there any areas God is wanting to grow my faith or trust?
Are there any insights from this week's work on how to do this?

Are there any sins God is spotlighting in my life?
Are there any insights from this week's work on how to kill these sins?

Re-read one or two of the most impactful verses from this week and turn them into a prayer. (There is room on the next pages to write it down if you want.)

How can I thank or praise God as a result of what I've learned this week?

How can I apply what I've learned this week to my life today and next week?

Where do I need His strength for today? Tomorrow? Next week?

Is there a verse from this week that I should commit to memory? Write it on the next page or on a 3x5 card to take with you to memorize.

Are there any sins I need to confess to God in prayer?

Is there anyone I need to forgive? Is there anyone I need to ask forgiveness of?

Are there any seeds of bitterness starting to take root in my heart?

Are there any fears or worries I need to lay at His feet?

notes, verses to memorize

prayers, doodles, etc

Joshua 19

Date:

Summarize the main idea(s) in this chapter:

Verse(s) that stood out 　　　　or　　　　Who is in this chapter?
What do they say? What do they do?

Why did I pick this verse? 　　　　or　　　　What is going on?
Is there anything going wrong?

Definitions of words and/or 　　　　or　　　　When and where
cross references from my verse 　　　　　　　　　did this happen?

Rewrite the passage in your own words   or   Why is this chapter in the Bible?
or personalize it.   Why did these events happen?
                                                                 Why did the people act this way?

Does this reveal anything about God/Jesus/Holy Spirit?
Are there examples to follow or avoid? What does this chapter have to teach me?

How can I apply insights from this today? This week?

Notes, quotes, doodles, checklists, prayers, etc.

Joshua 20

Date:

Summarize the main idea(s) in this chapter:

_____
_____
_____
_____

Verse(s) that stood out   or   Who is in this chapter?
What do they say? What do they do?

_____
_____
_____
_____
_____
_____

Why did I pick this verse?   or   What is going on?
Is there anything going wrong?

_____
_____
_____
_____

Definitions of words and/or   or   When and where
cross references from my verse   did this happen?

_____
_____
_____
_____
_____
_____
_____
_____

Rewrite the passage in your own words   or   Why is this chapter in the Bible?
or personalize it.   Why did these events happen?
                                                                        Why did the people act this way?

Does this reveal anything about God/Jesus/Holy Spirit?
Are there examples to follow or avoid? What does this chapter have to teach me?

How can I apply insights from this today? This week?

Notes, quotes, doodles, checklists, prayers, etc.

Joshua 21

Date:

Summarize the main idea(s) in this chapter:

Verse(s) that stood out   or   Who is in this chapter?
What do they say? What do they do?

Why did I pick this verse?   or   What is going on?
Is there anything going wrong?

Definitions of words and/or   or   When and where
cross references from my verse   did this happen?

Rewrite the passage in your own words   or   Why is this chapter in the Bible?
or personalize it.   Why did these events happen?
                                                               Why did the people act this way?

Does this reveal anything about God/Jesus/Holy Spirit?
Are there examples to follow or avoid? What does this chapter have to teach me?

How can I apply insights from this today? This week?

Notes, quotes, doodles, checklists, prayers, etc.

133

Joshua 22

Date:

Summarize the main idea(s) in this chapter:

Verse(s) that stood out   or   Who is in this chapter?
What do they say? What do they do?

Why did I pick this verse?   or   What is going on?
Is there anything going wrong?

Definitions of words and/or   or   When and where
cross references from my verse   did this happen?

Rewrite the passage in your own words or personalize it.

or

Why is this chapter in the Bible?
Why did these events happen?
Why did the people act this way?

Does this reveal anything about God/Jesus/Holy Spirit?
Are there examples to follow or avoid? What does this chapter have to teach me?

How can I apply insights from this today? This week?

Notes, quotes, doodles, checklists, prayers, etc.

Joshua 23-24

Date:

Summarize the main idea(s) in this chapter:

Verse(s) that stood out   or   Who is in this chapter?
What do they say? What do they do?

Why did I pick this verse?   or   What is going on?
Is there anything going wrong?

Definitions of words and/or   or   When and where
cross references from my verse   did this happen?

Rewrite the passage in your own words   or   Why is this chapter in the Bible?
or personalize it.   Why did these events happen?
                                                                      Why did the people act this way?

Does this reveal anything about God/Jesus/Holy Spirit?
Are there examples to follow or avoid? What does this chapter have to teach me?

How can I apply insights from this today? This week?

Notes, quotes, doodles, checklists, prayers, etc.

Review and reflect

Date:

Review each of the last six days work. Write or list the main takeaway you got from each chapter. (Look closely at the sections "What does this reveal about God?" and "How can I apply this?")

Are there any themes showing up in this week's work?

Are there any areas God is wanting to grow my faith or trust?
Are there any insights from this week's work on how to do this?

Are there any sins God is spotlighting in my life?
Are there any insights from this week's work on how to kill these sins?

Re-read one or two of the most impactful verses from this week and turn them into a prayer. (There is room on the next pages to write it down if you want.)

How can I thank or praise God as a result of what I've learned this week?

How can I apply what I've learned this week to my life today and next week?

Where do I need His strength for today? Tomorrow? Next week?

Is there a verse from this week that I should commit to memory? Write it on the next page or on a 3x5 card to take with you to memorize.

Are there any sins I need to confess to God in prayer?

Is there anyone I need to forgive? Is there anyone I need to ask forgiveness of?

Are there any seeds of bitterness starting to take root in my heart?

Are there any fears or worries I need to lay at His feet?

#Iwillmeditate

notes, verses to memorize

prayers, doodles, etc

the book of Romans preview

Read the introduction to the book of Romans in your Bible and jot down any notes.

There are some EXCELLENT videos on TheBibleProject.com or on their YouTube channel. On their website you can even print out a copy of their drawing (I shrink it down and print it out and tape it into my guide on the preview page). View the videos on the Bible project and also read the introduction at the beginning of the book in your Bible. They also have lots of other great resources, including podcasts talking about books of the Bible, so spend some time browsing around their site.

If you want to go even further, there are great free commentaries online to look up too. Here are some I love:

From Grace to You:
https://www.gty.org/library/bible-introductions

From Precept Austin:
http://www.preceptaustin.org/bybook

and Blue Letter Bible:
https://www.blueletterbible.org/resources/intros.cfm

Also, take a few moments to pray before you start your study:

my prayer

Romans preview notes

Rome

3 Taverns

ITALY

DALMATIA

MACEDONIA

Thessalonica

Puteoli

SICILY

ACHAIA
(GREECE)

Syracuse

Melita

Paul is taken prisoner to Rome

The GREAT

CR

Claud

TRIPOLIS

LIB

THRACE

BLACK SEA

BITHYNIA

ASIA

GALATIA

CAPPADOCIA

SYRIA

Rhodes

Myra

CYPRUS

Sidon

Fair Havens

Caesarea

Antipatris

Jerusalem

SEA

EGYPT

Browne

Romans 1

Date:

Summarize the main idea(s) in this chapter:

Verse(s) that stood out   or   Who is in this chapter?
What do they say? What do they do?

Why did I pick this verse?   or   What is going on?
Is there anything going wrong?

Definitions of words and/or   or   When and where
cross references from my verse   did this happen?

Rewrite the passage in your own words   or   Why is this chapter in the Bible?
or personalize it.   Why did these events happen?
                                                          Why did the people act this way?

Does this reveal anything about God/Jesus/Holy Spirit?
Are there examples to follow or avoid? What does this chapter have to teach me?

How can I apply insights from this today? This week?

Notes, quotes, doodles, checklists, prayers, etc.

Romans 2

Date:

Summarize the main idea(s) in this chapter:

Verse(s) that stood out   or   Who is in this chapter?
What do they say? What do they do?

Why did I pick this verse?   or   What is going on?
Is there anything going wrong?

Definitions of words and/or   or   When and where
cross references from my verse   did this happen?

Rewrite the passage in your own words   or   Why is this chapter in the Bible?
or personalize it.   Why did these events happen?
                                                 Why did the people act this way?

Does this reveal anything about God/Jesus/Holy Spirit?
Are there examples to follow or avoid? What does this chapter have to teach me?

How can I apply insights from this today? This week?

Notes, quotes, doodles, checklists, prayers, etc.

#Iwillmeditate

Romans 3

Date: _____

Summarize the main idea(s) in this chapter:

_____

_____

_____

_____

_____

Verse(s) that stood out	or	Who is in this chapter? What do they say? What do they do?

_____

_____

_____

_____

_____

Why did I pick this verse?	or	What is going on? Is there anything going wrong?

_____

_____

_____

_____

Definitions of words and/or cross references from my verse	or	When and where did this happen?

_____

_____

_____

_____

_____

_____

_____

_____

_____

Rewrite the passage in your own words   or   Why is this chapter in the Bible?
or personalize it.   Why did these events happen?
                                                Why did the people act this way?

Does this reveal anything about God/Jesus/Holy Spirit?
Are there examples to follow or avoid? What does this chapter have to teach me?

How can I apply insights from this today? This week?

Notes, quotes, doodles, checklists, prayers, etc.

Romans 4

Date: _____

Summarize the main idea(s) in this chapter:

_____

_____

_____

_____

_____

Verse(s) that stood out	or	Who is in this chapter? What do they say? What do they do?

_____

_____

_____

_____

_____

_____

Why did I pick this verse?	or	What is going on? Is there anything going wrong?

_____

_____

_____

_____

Definitions of words and/or cross references from my verse	or	When and where did this happen?

_____

_____

_____

_____

_____

_____

_____

_____

_____

_____

Rewrite the passage in your own words   or   Why is this chapter in the Bible?
or personalize it.   Why did these events happen?
                                                Why did the people act this way?

Does this reveal anything about God/Jesus/Holy Spirit?
Are there examples to follow or avoid? What does this chapter have to teach me?

How can I apply insights from this today? This week?

Notes, quotes, doodles, checklists, prayers, etc.

☐ pray before beginning
☐ review what came before

Romans 5

Date:

Summarize the main idea(s) in this chapter:

Verse(s) that stood out   or   Who is in this chapter?
What do they say? What do they do?

Why did I pick this verse?   or   What is going on?
Is there anything going wrong?

Definitions of words and/or   or   When and where
cross references from my verse   did this happen?

Rewrite the passage in your own words   or   Why is this chapter in the Bible?
or personalize it.   Why did these events happen?
                                                               Why did the people act this way?

Does this reveal anything about God/Jesus/Holy Spirit?
Are there examples to follow or avoid? What does this chapter have to teach me?

How can I apply insights from this today? This week?

Notes, quotes, doodles, checklists, prayers, etc.

Romans 6

Date:

Summarize the main idea(s) in this chapter:

Verse(s) that stood out   or   Who is in this chapter?
What do they say? What do they do?

Why did I pick this verse?   or   What is going on?
Is there anything going wrong?

Definitions of words and/or   or   When and where
cross references from my verse   did this happen?

Rewrite the passage in your own words   or   Why is this chapter in the Bible?
or personalize it.   Why did these events happen?
                                                            Why did the people act this way?

Does this reveal anything about God/Jesus/Holy Spirit?
Are there examples to follow or avoid? What does this chapter have to teach me?

How can I apply insights from this today? This week?

Notes, quotes, doodles, checklists, prayers, etc.

Review and reflect

Date:

Review each of the last six days work. Write or list the main takeaway you got from each chapter. (Look closely at the sections "What does this reveal about God?" and "How can I apply this?")

Are there any themes showing up in this week's work?

Are there any areas God is wanting to grow my faith or trust?
Are there any insights from this week's work on how to do this?

Are there any sins God is spotlighting in my life?
Are there any insights from this week's work on how to kill these sins?

Re-read one or two of the most impactful verses from this week and turn them into a prayer. (There is room on the next pages to write it down if you want.)

How can I thank or praise God as a result of what I've learned this week?

How can I apply what I've learned this week to my life today and next week?

Where do I need His strength for today? Tomorrow? Next week?

Is there a verse from this week that I should commit to memory? Write it on the next page or on a 3x5 card to take with you to memorize.

Are there any sins I need to confess to God in prayer?

Is there anyone I need to forgive? Is there anyone I need to ask forgiveness of?

Are there any seeds of bitterness starting to take root in my heart?

Are there any fears or worries I need to lay at His feet?

notes, verses to memorize

prayers, doodles, etc

Romans 7

Date:

Summarize the main idea(s) in this chapter:

Verse(s) that stood out   or   Who is in this chapter?
                                                          What do they say? What do they do?

Why did I pick this verse?   or   What is going on?
                                                          Is there anything going wrong?

Definitions of words and/or   or   When and where
cross references from my verse   did this happen?

Rewrite the passage in your own words   or   Why is this chapter in the Bible?
or personalize it.   Why did these events happen?
                                                           Why did the people act this way?

Does this reveal anything about God/Jesus/Holy Spirit?
Are there examples to follow or avoid? What does this chapter have to teach me?

How can I apply insights from this today? This week?

Notes, quotes, doodles, checklists, prayers, etc.

Romans 8

Date:

Summarize the main idea(s) in this chapter:

Verse(s) that stood out   or   Who is in this chapter?
What do they say? What do they do?

Why did I pick this verse?   or   What is going on?
Is there anything going wrong?

Definitions of words and/or   or   When and where
cross references from my verse   did this happen?

Rewrite the passage in your own words   or   Why is this chapter in the Bible?
or personalize it.   Why did these events happen?
                                                               Why did the people act this way?

Does this reveal anything about God/Jesus/Holy Spirit?
Are there examples to follow or avoid? What does this chapter have to teach me?

How can I apply insights from this today? This week?

Notes, quotes, doodles, checklists, prayers, etc.

#Iwillmeditate

☐ pray before beginning
☐ review what came before

Romans 9

Date:

Summarize the main idea(s) in this chapter:

Verse(s) that stood out   or   Who is in this chapter?
What do they say? What do they do?

Why did I pick this verse?   or   What is going on?
Is there anything going wrong?

Definitions of words and/or   or   When and where
cross references from my verse   did this happen?

Rewrite the passage in your own words   or   Why is this chapter in the Bible?
or personalize it.   Why did these events happen?
                                                Why did the people act this way?

Does this reveal anything about God/Jesus/Holy Spirit?
Are there examples to follow or avoid? What does this chapter have to teach me?

How can I apply insights from this today? This week?

Notes, quotes, doodles, checklists, prayers, etc.

#Iwillmeditate

Romans 10

Date:

Summarize the main idea(s) in this chapter:

Verse(s) that stood out   or   Who is in this chapter?
What do they say? What do they do?

Why did I pick this verse?   or   What is going on?
Is there anything going wrong?

Definitions of words and/or   or   When and where
cross references from my verse   did this happen?

Rewrite the passage in your own words   or   Why is this chapter in the Bible?
or personalize it.   Why did these events happen?
                                                                    Why did the people act this way?

Does this reveal anything about God/Jesus/Holy Spirit?
Are there examples to follow or avoid? What does this chapter have to teach me?

How can I apply insights from this today? This week?

Notes, quotes, doodles, checklists, prayers, etc.

#Iwillmeditate

☐ pray before beginning
☐ review what came before

Romans 11

Date:

Summarize the main idea(s) in this chapter:

Verse(s) that stood out   or   Who is in this chapter?
What do they say? What do they do?

Why did I pick this verse?   or   What is going on?
Is there anything going wrong?

Definitions of words and/or   or   When and where
cross references from my verse   did this happen?

Rewrite the passage in your own words   or   Why is this chapter in the Bible?
or personalize it.   Why did these events happen?
                                                                      Why did the people act this way?

Does this reveal anything about God/Jesus/Holy Spirit?
Are there examples to follow or avoid? What does this chapter have to teach me?

How can I apply insights from this today? This week?

Notes, quotes, doodles, checklists, prayers, etc.

Romans 12

Date:

Summarize the main idea(s) in this chapter:

Verse(s) that stood out   or   Who is in this chapter?
What do they say? What do they do?

Why did I pick this verse?   or   What is going on?
Is there anything going wrong?

Definitions of words and/or   or   When and where
cross references from my verse   did this happen?

Rewrite the passage in your own words   or   Why is this chapter in the Bible?
or personalize it.   Why did these events happen?
                                                   Why did the people act this way?

Does this reveal anything about God/Jesus/Holy Spirit?
Are there examples to follow or avoid? What does this chapter have to teach me?

How can I apply insights from this today? This week?

Notes, quotes, doodles, checklists, prayers, etc.

Review and reflect

Date:

Review each of the last six days work. Write or list the main takeaway you got from each chapter. (Look closely at the sections "What does this reveal about God?" and "How can I apply this?")

Are there any themes showing up in this week's work?

Are there any areas God is wanting to grow my faith or trust?
Are there any insights from this week's work on how to do this?

Are there any sins God is spotlighting in my life?
Are there any insights from this week's work on how to kill these sins?

Re-read one or two of the most impactful verses from this week and turn them into a prayer. (There is room on the next pages to write it down if you want.)

How can I thank or praise God as a result of what I've learned this week?

How can I apply what I've learned this week to my life today and next week?

Where do I need His strength for today? Tomorrow? Next week?

Is there a verse from this week that I should commit to memory? Write it on the next page or on a 3x5 card to take with you to memorize.

Are there any sins I need to confess to God in prayer?

Is there anyone I need to forgive? Is there anyone I need to ask forgiveness of?

Are there any seeds of bitterness starting to take root in my heart?

Are there any fears or worries I need to lay at His feet?

notes, verses to memorize

prayers, doodles, etc

☐ pray before beginning
☐ review what came before

Romans 13

Date:

Summarize the main idea(s) in this chapter:

Verse(s) that stood out   or   Who is in this chapter?
What do they say? What do they do?

Why did I pick this verse?   or   What is going on?
Is there anything going wrong?

Definitions of words and/or   or   When and where
cross references from my verse   did this happen?

Rewrite the passage in your own words   or   Why is this chapter in the Bible?
or personalize it.   Why did these events happen?
                                                               Why did the people act this way?

Does this reveal anything about God/Jesus/Holy Spirit?
Are there examples to follow or avoid? What does this chapter have to teach me?

How can I apply insights from this today? This week?

Notes, quotes, doodles, checklists, prayers, etc.

Romans 14

Date:

Summarize the main idea(s) in this chapter:

Verse(s) that stood out   or   Who is in this chapter?
What do they say? What do they do?

Why did I pick this verse?   or   What is going on?
Is there anything going wrong?

Definitions of words and/or   or   When and where
cross references from my verse   did this happen?

Rewrite the passage in your own words   or   Why is this chapter in the Bible?
or personalize it.   Why did these events happen?
                                                                            Why did the people act this way?

Does this reveal anything about God/Jesus/Holy Spirit?
Are there examples to follow or avoid? What does this chapter have to teach me?

How can I apply insights from this today? This week?

Notes, quotes, doodles, checklists, prayers, etc.

☐ pray before beginning
☐ review what came before

Romans 15

Date:

Summarize the main idea(s) in this chapter:

Verse(s) that stood out   or   Who is in this chapter?
What do they say? What do they do?

Why did I pick this verse?   or   What is going on?
Is there anything going wrong?

Definitions of words and/or   or   When and where
cross references from my verse   did this happen?

Rewrite the passage in your own words
or personalize it.

or

Why is this chapter in the Bible?
Why did these events happen?
Why did the people act this way?

Does this reveal anything about God/Jesus/Holy Spirit?
Are there examples to follow or avoid? What does this chapter have to teach me?

How can I apply insights from this today? This week?

Notes, quotes, doodles, checklists, prayers, etc.

#Iwillmeditate

pray before beginning
review what came before

Romans 16

Date:

Summarize the main idea(s) in this chapter:

Verse(s) that stood out   or   Who is in this chapter?
What do they say? What do they do?

Why did I pick this verse?   or   What is going on?
Is there anything going wrong?

Definitions of words and/or   or   When and where
cross references from my verse   did this happen?

Rewrite the passage in your own words   or   Why is this chapter in the Bible?
or personalize it.   Why did these events happen?
                                                                      Why did the people act this way?

Does this reveal anything about God/Jesus/Holy Spirit?
Are there examples to follow or avoid? What does this chapter have to teach me?

How can I apply insights from this today? This week?

Notes, quotes, doodles, checklists, prayers, etc.

Review and reflect

Date:

Review each of the last six days work. Write or list the main takeaway you got from each chapter. (Look closely at the sections "What does this reveal about God?" and "How can I apply this?")

Are there any themes showing up in this week's work?

Are there any areas God is wanting to grow my faith or trust?
Are there any insights from this week's work on how to do this?

Are there any sins God is spotlighting in my life?
Are there any insights from this week's work on how to kill these sins?

Re-read one or two of the most impactful verses from this week and turn them into a prayer. (There is room on the next pages to write it down if you want.)

How can I thank or praise God as a result of what I've learned this week?

How can I apply what I've learned this week to my life today and next week?

Where do I need His strength for today? Tomorrow? Next week?

Is there a verse from this week that I should commit to memory? Write it on the next page or on a 3x5 card to take with you to memorize.

Are there any sins I need to confess to God in prayer?

Is there anyone I need to forgive? Is there anyone I need to ask forgiveness of?

Are there any seeds of bitterness starting to take root in my heart?

Are there any fears or worries I need to lay at His feet?

notes, verses to memorize

prayers, doodles, etc

The book of Judges preview

Read the introduction to the book of Judges in your Bible and jot down any notes.

There are some EXCELLENT videos on TheBibleProject.com or on their YouTube channel. On their website you can even print out a copy of their drawing (I shrink it down and print it out and tape it into my guide on the preview page). View the videos on the Bible project and also read the introduction at the beginning of the book in your Bible. They also have lots of other great resources, including podcasts talking about books of the Bible, so spend some time browsing around their site.

If you want to go even further, there are great free commentaries online to look up too. Here are some I love:

From Grace to You:
https://www.gty.org/library/bible-introductions

From Precept Austin:
http://www.preceptaustin.org/bybook

And Blue Letter Bible:
https://www.blueletterbible.org/resources/intros.cfm

Also, take a few moments to pray before you start your study:

my prayer

Judges preview notes

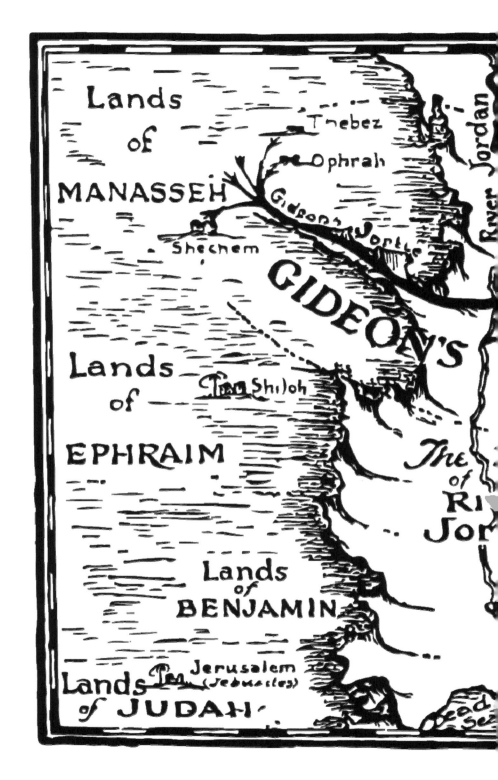

Lands
of

GILEAD

Succoth.

R Jabbok

Jabbok

Hostile Tribes

REALM

Penuel

The Midianites Flee

Ravine
he
er
dan

Lands
of
GAD

Hostile Tribes

Lands of
REUBEN

B. wne

Judges 1

Date:

Summarize the main idea(s) in this chapter:

Verse(s) that stood out   or   Who is in this chapter?
What do they say? What do they do?

Why did I pick this verse?   or   What is going on?
Is there anything going wrong?

Definitions of words and/or   or   When and where
cross references from my verse   did this happen?

Rewrite the passage in your own words   or   Why is this chapter in the Bible?
or personalize it.   Why did these events happen?
                                                                      Why did the people act this way?

Does this reveal anything about God/Jesus/Holy Spirit?
Are there examples to follow or avoid? What does this chapter have to teach me?

How can I apply insights from this today? This week?

Notes, quotes, doodles, checklists, prayers, etc.

Judges 2

Date:

Summarize the main idea(s) in this chapter:

Verse(s) that stood out   or   Who is in this chapter?
What do they say? What do they do?

Why did I pick this verse?   or   What is going on?
Is there anything going wrong?

Definitions of words and/or   or   When and where
cross references from my verse   did this happen?

Rewrite the passage in your own words   or   Why is this chapter in the Bible?
or personalize it.   Why did these events happen?
                                                                  Why did the people act this way?

Does this reveal anything about God/Jesus/Holy Spirit?
Are there examples to follow or avoid? What does this chapter have to teach me?

How can I apply insights from this today? This week?

Notes, quotes, doodles, checklists, prayers, etc.

#Iwillmeditate

Judges 3

Date:

Summarize the main idea(s) in this chapter:

Verse(s) that stood out   or   Who is in this chapter?
What do they say? What do they do?

Why did I pick this verse?   or   What is going on?
Is there anything going wrong?

Definitions of words and/or   or   When and where
cross references from my verse   did this happen?

Rewrite the passage in your own words   or   Why is this chapter in the Bible?
or personalize it.   Why did these events happen?
                                                                                 Why did the people act this way?

Does this reveal anything about God/Jesus/Holy Spirit?
Are there examples to follow or avoid? What does this chapter have to teach me?

How can I apply insights from this today? This week?

Notes, quotes, doodles, checklists, prayers, etc.

Judges 4

Date:

Summarize the main idea(s) in this chapter:

Verse(s) that stood out   or   Who is in this chapter?
What do they say? What do they do?

Why did I pick this verse?   or   What is going on?
Is there anything going wrong?

Definitions of words and/or   or   When and where
cross references from my verse   did this happen?

Rewrite the passage in your own words   or   Why is this chapter in the Bible?
or personalize it.   Why did these events happen?
                                                                          Why did the people act this way?

Does this reveal anything about God/Jesus/Holy Spirit?
Are there examples to follow or avoid? What does this chapter have to teach me?

How can I apply insights from this today? This week?

Notes, quotes, doodles, checklists, prayers, etc.

#Iwillmeditate

☐ pray before beginning
☐ review what came before

Judges 5

Date:

Summarize the main idea(s) in this chapter:

Verse(s) that stood out   or   Who is in this chapter?
What do they say? What do they do?

Why did I pick this verse?   or   What is going on?
Is there anything going wrong?

Definitions of words and/or   or   When and where
cross references from my verse   did this happen?

Rewrite the passage in your own words   or   Why is this chapter in the Bible?
or personalize it.   Why did these events happen?
                                                                 Why did the people act this way?

Does this reveal anything about God/Jesus/Holy Spirit?
Are there examples to follow or avoid? What does this chapter have to teach me?

How can I apply insights from this today? This week?

Notes, quotes, doodles, checklists, prayers, etc.

207

Judges 6

Date:

Summarize the main idea(s) in this chapter:

Verse(s) that stood out   or   Who is in this chapter?
What do they say? What do they do?

Why did I pick this verse?   or   What is going on?
Is there anything going wrong?

Definitions of words and/or   or   When and where
cross references from my verse   did this happen?

Rewrite the passage in your own words   or   Why is this chapter in the Bible?
or personalize it.   Why did these events happen?
                                                                           Why did the people act this way?

Does this reveal anything about God/Jesus/Holy Spirit?
Are there examples to follow or avoid? What does this chapter have to teach me?

How can I apply insights from this today? This week?

Notes, quotes, doodles, checklists, prayers, etc.

Review and reflect

Date:

Review each of the last six days work. Write or list the main takeaway you got from each chapter. (Look closely at the sections "What does this reveal about God?" and "How can I apply this?")

Are there any themes showing up in this week's work?

Are there any areas God is wanting to grow my faith or trust?
Are there any insights from this week's work on how to do this?

Are there any sins God is spotlighting in my life?
Are there any insights from this week's work on how to kill these sins?

Re-read one or two of the most impactful verses from this week and turn them into a prayer. (There is room on the next pages to write it down if you want.)

How can I thank or praise God as a result of what I've learned this week?

How can I apply what I've learned this week to my life today and next week?

Where do I need His strength for today? Tomorrow? Next week?

Is there a verse from this week that I should commit to memory? Write it on the next page or on a 3x5 card to take with you to memorize.

Are there any sins I need to confess to God in prayer?

Is there anyone I need to forgive? Is there anyone I need to ask forgiveness of?

Are there any seeds of bitterness starting to take root in my heart?

Are there any fears or worries I need to lay at His feet?

notes, verses to memorize

prayers, doodles, etc

☐ pray before beginning
☐ review what came before

Judges 7

Date:

Summarize the main idea(s) in this chapter:

Verse(s) that stood out   or   Who is in this chapter?
What do they say? What do they do?

Why did I pick this verse?   or   What is going on?
Is there anything going wrong?

Definitions of words and/or   or   When and where
cross references from my verse   did this happen?

Rewrite the passage in your own words   or   Why is this chapter in the Bible?
or personalize it.   Why did these events happen?
                                                                      Why did the people act this way?

Does this reveal anything about God/Jesus/Holy Spirit?
Are there examples to follow or avoid? What does this chapter have to teach me?

How can I apply insights from this today? This week?

Notes, quotes, doodles, checklists, prayers, etc.

#Iwillmeditate

Judges 8

Date:

Summarize the main idea(s) in this chapter:

Verse(s) that stood out   or   Who is in this chapter?
What do they say? What do they do?

Why did I pick this verse?   or   What is going on?
Is there anything going wrong?

Definitions of words and/or   or   When and where
cross references from my verse   did this happen?

Rewrite the passage in your own words   or   Why is this chapter in the Bible?
or personalize it.   Why did these events happen?
                                                                           Why did the people act this way?

Does this reveal anything about God/Jesus/Holy Spirit?
Are there examples to follow or avoid? What does this chapter have to teach me?

How can I apply insights from this today? This week?

Notes, quotes, doodles, checklists, prayers, etc.

Judges 9

Date:

Summarize the main idea(s) in this chapter:

Verse(s) that stood out   or   Who is in this chapter?
What do they say? What do they do?

Why did I pick this verse?   or   What is going on?
Is there anything going wrong?

Definitions of words and/or   or   When and where
cross references from my verse   did this happen?

Rewrite the passage in your own words   or   Why is this chapter in the Bible?
or personalize it.   Why did these events happen?
                                                             Why did the people act this way?

Does this reveal anything about God/Jesus/Holy Spirit?
Are there examples to follow or avoid? What does this chapter have to teach me?

How can I apply insights from this today? This week?

Notes, quotes, doodles, checklists, prayers, etc.

Judges 10

Date:

Summarize the main idea(s) in this chapter:

Verse(s) that stood out   or   Who is in this chapter?
What do they say? What do they do?

Why did I pick this verse?   or   What is going on?
Is there anything going wrong?

Definitions of words and/or   or   When and where
cross references from my verse   did this happen?

Rewrite the passage in your own words   or   Why is this chapter in the Bible?
or personalize it.   Why did these events happen?
                                                                           Why did the people act this way?

Does this reveal anything about God/Jesus/Holy Spirit?
Are there examples to follow or avoid? What does this chapter have to teach me?

How can I apply insights from this today? This week?

Notes, quotes, doodles, checklists, prayers, etc.

Judges 11

Date:

Summarize the main idea(s) in this chapter:

Verse(s) that stood out   or   Who is in this chapter?
What do they say? What do they do?

Why did I pick this verse?   or   What is going on
Is there anything going wrong?

Definitions of words and/or   or   When and where
cross references from my verse   did this happen?

Rewrite the passage in your own words   or   Why is this chapter in the Bible?
or personalize it.   Why did these events happen?
                                                                        Why did the people act this way?

Does this reveal anything about God/Jesus/Holy Spirit?
Are there examples to follow or avoid? What does this chapter have to teach me?

How can I apply insights from this today? This week?

Notes, quotes, doodles, checklists, prayers, etc.

223

☐ pray before beginning
☐ review what came before

Judges 12-13

Date:

Summarize the main idea(s) in this chapter:

Verse(s) that stood out   or   Who is in this chapter?
What do they say? What do they do?

Why did I pick this verse?   or   What is going on?
Is there anything going wrong?

Definitions of words and/or   or   When and where
cross references from my verse   did this happen?

224

Rewrite the passage in your own words   or   Why is this chapter in the Bible?
or personalize it.   Why did these events happen?
                                                Why did the people act this way?

Does this reveal anything about God/Jesus/Holy Spirit?
Are there examples to follow or avoid? What does this chapter have to teach me?

How can I apply insights from this today? This week?

Notes, quotes, doodles, checklists, prayers, etc.

☐ pray before beginning

Review and reflect

Date:

Review each of the last six days work. Write or list the main takeaway you got from each chapter. (Look closely at the sections "What does this reveal about God?" and "How can I apply this?")

Are there any themes showing up in this week's work?

Are there any areas God is wanting to grow my faith or trust?
Are there any insights from this week's work on how to do this?

Are there any sins God is spotlighting in my life?
Are there any insights from this week's work on how to kill these sins?

Re-read one or two of the most impactful verses from this week and turn them into a prayer. (There is room on the next pages to write it down if you want.)

How can I thank or praise God as a result of what I've learned this week?

How can I apply what I've learned this week to my life today and next week?

Where do I need His strength for today? Tomorrow? Next week?

Is there a verse from this week that I should commit to memory? Write it on the next page or on a 3x5 card to take with you to memorize.

Are there any sins I need to confess to God in prayer?

Is there anyone I need to forgive? Is there anyone I need to ask forgiveness of?

Are there any seeds of bitterness starting to take root in my heart?

Are there any fears or worries I need to lay at His feet?

notes, verses to memorize

prayers, doodles, etc

Judges 14-15

Date:

Summarize the main idea(s) in this chapter:

Verse(s) that stood out   or   Who is in this chapter?
What do they say? What do they do?

Why did I pick this verse?   or   What is going on?
Is there anything going wrong?

Definitions of words and/or   or   When and where
cross references from my verse   did this happen?

Rewrite the passage in your own words   or   Why is this chapter in the Bible?
or personalize it.   Why did these events happen?
                                                                     Why did the people act this way?

Does this reveal anything about God/Jesus/Holy Spirit?
Are there examples to follow or avoid? What does this chapter have to teach me?

How can I apply insights from this today? This week?

Notes, quotes, doodles, checklists, prayers, etc.

#Iwillmeditate

Judges 16-17

Date:

Summarize the main idea(s) in this chapter:

Verse(s) that stood out   or   Who is in this chapter?
What do they say? What do they do?

Why did I pick this verse?   or   What is going on?
Is there anything going wrong?

Definitions of words and/or   or   When and where
cross references from my verse   did this happen?

Rewrite the passage in your own words   or   Why is this chapter in the Bible?
or personalize it.   Why did these events happen?
                                                                        Why did the people act this way?

Does this reveal anything about God/Jesus/Holy Spirit?
Are there examples to follow or avoid? What does this chapter have to teach me?

How can I apply insights from this today? This week?

Notes, quotes, doodles, checklists, prayers, etc.

Judges 18

Date:

Summarize the main idea(s) in this chapter:

Verse(s) that stood out   or   Who is in this chapter?
What do they say? What do they do?

Why did I pick this verse?   or   What is going on?
Is there anything going wrong?

Definitions of words and/or   or   When and where
cross references from my verse   did this happen?

Rewrite the passage in your own words   or   Why is this chapter in the Bible?
or personalize it.   Why did these events happen?
                                                                              Why did the people act this way?

Does this reveal anything about God/Jesus/Holy Spirit?
Are there examples to follow or avoid? What does this chapter have to teach me?

How can I apply insights from this today? This week?

Notes, quotes, doodles, checklists, prayers, etc.

#Iwillmeditate

☐ pray before beginning
☐ review what came before

Judges 19

Date:

Summarize the main idea(s) in this chapter:

Verse(s) that stood out   or   Who is in this chapter?
What do they say? What do they do?

Why did I pick this verse?   or   What is going on?
Is there anything going wrong?

Definitions of words and/or
cross references from my verse   or   When and where
did this happen?

Rewrite the passage in your own words   or   Why is this chapter in the Bible?
or personalize it.   Why did these events happen?
                                                    Why did the people act this way?

Does this reveal anything about God/Jesus/Holy Spirit?
Are there examples to follow or avoid? What does this chapter have to teach me?

How can I apply insights from this today? This week?

Notes, quotes, doodles, checklists, prayers, etc.

#Iwillmeditate

Judges 20

Date:

Summarize the main idea(s) in this chapter:

Verse(s) that stood out   or   Who is in this chapter?
What do they say? What do they do?

Why did I pick this verse?   or   What is going on?
Is there anything going wrong?

Definitions of words and/or   or   When and where
cross references from my verse   did this happen?

Rewrite the passage in your own words   or   Why is this chapter in the Bible?
or personalize it.   Why did these events happen?
                                                Why did the people act this way?

Does this reveal anything about God/Jesus/Holy Spirit?
Are there examples to follow or avoid? What does this chapter have to teach me?

How can I apply insights from this today? This week?

Notes, quotes, doodles, checklists, prayers, etc.

Judges 21

Date:

Summarize the main idea(s) in this chapter:

Verse(s) that stood out   or   Who is in this chapter?
What do they say? What do they do?

Why did I pick this verse?   or   What is going on?
Is there anything going wrong?

Definitions of words and/or   or   When and where
cross references from my verse   did this happen?

Rewrite the passage in your own words   or   Why is this chapter in the Bible?
or personalize it.   Why did these events happen?
                                                                          Why did the people act this way?

Does this reveal anything about God/Jesus/Holy Spirit?
Are there examples to follow or avoid? What does this chapter have to teach me?

How can I apply insights from this today? This week?

Notes, quotes, doodles, checklists, prayers, etc.

Review and reflect

Date:

Review each of the last six days work. Write or list the main takeaway you got from each chapter. (Look closely at the sections "What does this reveal about God?" and "How can I apply this?")

Are there any themes showing up in this week's work?

Are there any areas God is wanting to grow my faith or trust?
Are there any insights from this week's work on how to do this?

Are there any sins God is spotlighting in my life?
Are there any insights from this week's work on how to kill these sins?

Re-read one or two of the most impactful verses from this week and turn them into a prayer. (There is room on the next pages to write it down if you want.)

How can I thank or praise God as a result of what I've learned this week?

How can I apply what I've learned this week to my life today and next week?

Where do I need His strength for today? Tomorrow? Next week?

Is there a verse from this week that I should commit to memory? Write it on the next page or on a 3x5 card to take with you to memorize.

Are there any sins I need to confess to God in prayer?

Is there anyone I need to forgive? Is there anyone I need to ask forgiveness of?

Are there any seeds of bitterness starting to take root in my heart?

Are there any fears or worries I need to lay at His feet?

notes, verses to memorize

prayers, doodles, etc

the book of Ruth preview

Read the introduction to the book of Ruth in your Bible and jot down any notes.

There are some EXCELLENT videos on TheBibleProject.com or on their YouTube channel. On their website you can even print out a copy of their drawing (I shrink it down and print it out and tape it into my guide on the preview page). View the videos on the Bible project and also read the introduction at the beginning of the book in your Bible. They also have lots of other great resources, including podcasts talking about books of the Bible, so spend some time browsing around their site.

If you want to go even further, there are great free commentaries online to look up too. Here are some I love:

From Grace to You:
https://www.gty.org/library/bible-introductions

From Precept Austin:
http://www.preceptaustin.org/bybook

and Blue Letter Bible:
https://www.blueletterbible.org/resources/intros.cfm

Also, take a few moments to pray before you start your study:

my prayer

Ruth preview notes

Ruth 1

Date:

Summarize the main idea(s) in this chapter:

Verse(s) that stood out   or   Who is in this chapter?
What do they say? What do they do?

Why did I pick this verse?   or   What is going on?
Is there anything going wrong?

Definitions of words and/or
cross references from my verse   or   When and where
did this happen?

Rewrite the passage in your own words   or   Why is this chapter in the Bible?
or personalize it.   Why did these events happen?
                                                   Why did the people act this way?

Does this reveal anything about God/Jesus/Holy Spirit?
Are there examples to follow or avoid? What does this chapter have to teach me?

How can I apply insights from this today? This week?

Notes, quotes, doodles, checklists, prayers, etc.

#Iwillmeditate

Ruth 2

Date:

Summarize the main idea(s) in this chapter:

Verse(s) that stood out   or   Who is in this chapter?
What do they say? What do they do?

Why did I pick this verse?   or   What is going on?
Is there anything going wrong?

Definitions of words and/or   or   When and where
cross references from my verse   did this happen?

Rewrite the passage in your own words   or   Why is this chapter in the Bible?
or personalize it.   Why did these events happen?
                                                                      Why did the people act this way?

Does this reveal anything about God/Jesus/Holy Spirit?
Are there examples to follow or avoid? What does this chapter have to teach me?

How can I apply insights from this today? This week?

Notes, quotes, doodles, checklists, prayers, etc.

Ruth 3

Date:

Summarize the main idea(s) in this chapter:

Verse(s) that stood out   or   Who is in this chapter?
What do they say? What do they do?

Why did I pick this verse?   or   What is going on?
Is there anything going wrong?

Definitions of words and/or   or   When and where
cross references from my verse   did this happen?

Rewrite the passage in your own words   or   Why is this chapter in the Bible?
or personalize it.   Why did these events happen?
                                                                             Why did the people act this way?

Does this reveal anything about God/Jesus/Holy Spirit?
Are there examples to follow or avoid? What does this chapter have to teach me?

How can I apply insights from this today? This week?

Notes, quotes, doodles, checklists, prayers, etc.

Ruth 4

Date:

Summarize the main idea(s) in this chapter:

Verse(s) that stood out   or   Who is in this chapter?
What do they say? What do they do?

Why did I pick this verse?   or   What is going on?
Is there anything going wrong?

Definitions of words and/or   or   When and where
cross references from my verse   did this happen?

Rewrite the passage in your own words   or   Why is this chapter in the Bible?
or personalize it.   Why did these events happen?
                                                Why did the people act this way?

Does this reveal anything about God/Jesus/Holy Spirit?
Are there examples to follow or avoid? What does this chapter have to teach me?

How can I apply insights from this today? This week?

Notes, quotes, doodles, checklists, prayers, etc.

#Iwillmeditate

Review and reflect

Date:

Review each of the last six days work. Write or list the main takeaway you got from each chapter. (Look closely at the sections "What does this reveal about God?" and "How can I apply this?")

Are there any themes showing up in this week's work?

Are there any areas God is wanting to grow my faith or trust?
Are there any insights from this week's work on how to do this?

Are there any sins God is spotlighting in my life?
Are there any insights from this week's work on how to kill these sins?

Re-read one or two of the most impactful verses from this week and turn them into a prayer. (There is room on the next pages to write it down if you want.)

How can I thank or praise God as a result of what I've learned this week?

How can I apply what I've learned this week to my life today and next week?

Where do I need His strength for today? Tomorrow? Next week?

Is there a verse from this week that I should commit to memory? Write it on the next page or on a 3x5 card to take with you to memorize.

Are there any sins I need to confess to God in prayer?

Is there anyone I need to forgive? Is there anyone I need to ask forgiveness of?

Are there any seeds of bitterness starting to take root in my heart?

Are there any fears or worries I need to lay at His feet?

notes, verses to memorize

prayers, doodles, etc

Congratulations!

You did it! Great job on finishing. Look for Volume Five on Amazon to continue your journey through the Bible!

Also be sure to check out the Journal and Doodle Bible studies on Amazon and on my website www.StoneSoupforFive.com. These inductive Bible studies work through a book of the Bible and have questions to help you meditate, questions to answer, doodles, and much more.

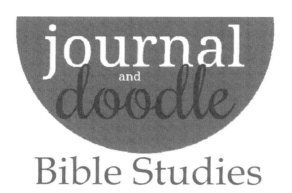

Bible Studies

www.StoneSoupforFive.com

Made in the USA
Middletown, DE
20 March 2020